About this book...

Best of British covers uniquely British traditions such as pantomime and Guy Fawke's Night; things that make a nation proud such as Wimbledon, fish and chips and Dame Vera Lynn. This book also looks at the 'traditions' that are uniquely British for all the wrong reasons: picnics in a car park, Morris dancers and mushy peas.

It identifies key areas the British will never understand, such as tipping waiters, long range weather forecasts, the national flag, and why socks shouldn't be worn with sandals. Also included are some of the things the British choose to ignore, such as the French, driving on the right and hosepipe bans.

Take note of the following:

1) The British take queueing very seriously.

2) The English language provides an enormous choice of colourful metaphors to use in unsatisfactory situations.

So, why is engaging in dialogue with a queue-jumping chancer at the airport check-in simply 'not British'?!

In such an 'unsatisfactory situation', why do the British choose, instead, to express their displeasure via a rather sophisticated 'sub-language' of tuts and sighs, applied at varying degrees of volume? Similarly, why does watching somebody in the 'ten items or less' checkout with an overflowing trolley warrant a 'treble tut and head-shake combo'?

And, if the British are world leaders in queueing politely, why doesn't this ever apply when driving, at car boot sales or when trying to board a train before 9am in the morning?

And if you don't find Best of British funny, wrap it up and give it to Uncle Gordon next Christmas.

3

A small holding...
...or large marrow?

Approximately 784,000 Britons have allotments. The average British allotment is big enough for thirteen bamboo canes covered with upturned plastic containers. And a shed. If all the runner beans produced from these small holdings were put end to end they would reach into outer-space…which would be a monumentally pointless task eqivalent to noodling around with their courgettes on an allotment.

Evidently, there is nothing more satisfying than proudly announcing to your dinner guests that the reason they've got jaw ache from chewing what appears to be green string for the last ten minutes is that the runner beans are 'from the allotment'. Taking just a few months to grow and saving £1.10, the enjoyment doesn't end there, either. The allotment shed also has the added benefit of being one of the last remaining safe havens for the British male, after the Working Men's Club and The Pink Pussycat (closed Wednesdays).

BEST of BRITISH

igloo

Published in 2008
by Igloo Books Ltd
Cottage Farm
Sywell
NN6 0BJ
www.igloo-books.com
Copyright © 2008 Igloo Books Ltd

10 9 8 7 6 5 4 3 2 1

ISBN: 978-1-84817-133-6

Designed by 2h Design

Printed and manufactured in China

This year, Ernie Wilson's allotment produced four carrots, an undersized parsnip and backache

Accents
Regional dialects; English as a second language

A survey on behalf of UK call centres, outsourced to the Philippines, revealed the most popular regional accents are from Liverpool, Glasgow, Belfast and Wolverhampton. All were perceived to be trusting, honest and understanding. Results showed that the Scouse accent was furest (fairest), whereas the Glaswegian accent is compulsory when telling the following joke;

McDougal is weaving unsteadily down Argyle Street when he spots a man under the bonnet of a car…

'What's up Jimmy?'

'Piston broke'

'Aye, same here'.

Anorak
(or 'cagoule' from the French word meaning ridiculous')

Type of not-quite waterproof jacket and retro fashion essential for Britain's 35 million ramblers and train botherers. Constructed from a lightweight plastic based material, it cleverly allows rain to slowly penetrate whilst the body becomes increasingly hot and sweaty due to lack of ventilation. Available in a wide choice of bright or very bright colours, including Golden Sunburst, Avocado Sorbet, Mediterranean Azure and Red Squirrel.

Beach Huts
Sheds with a sea view

A common sight on the foreshore and promenade of many British seaside resorts is that of the beach hut. This brightly painted variant of the garden shed, usually sporting a rusty padlock and partly collapsed roof, has a multitude of uses. Despite not benefiting from running water or electricity and costing a fortune to rent, the beach hut retains a primary function to store 'beach paraphernalia'.

Reclining loungers, wind breaks, sun umbrellas and deckchairs happily sit alongside an inflatable killer whale, a yellow flip flop and a dinghy paddle. A Calor gas primus stove, two chipped mugs, an arm band and collection of stones in a small plastic bucket are all neatly stacked inside the hut, ready and waiting for the next sunny day at the beach. Which explains the rusty padlock.

Contents of average UK beach hut

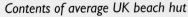

Bingo
Eyes down and looking

The game of *Bingo* or *Housey Housey* has been played for as long as elderly ladies have had *Housey Housey* or bingo wings. There are over 400 registered Bingo Halls in Britain where linked prizes of up to £500,000 can be won. An average game takes about five minutes, making it an ideal 'between naps' pastime.

The professional bingo caller will often announce a traditional catchphrase before calling both digits on their own eg: '4 and 4: Droopy Draws', '8 and 3: Time for Tea'.

The call for 47, '4 and 7: Four and Seven' has been criticised for its lack of imagination. In 1986 ('Goodbye Teens' and 'Between the Sticks') a group of Bingo enthusiasts from Lyme Regis lobbied for the rhyme to be changed from Four and Seven to 'Lyme Regis, Dorset not very far from Devon'. This was quickly ruled out by two ladies from UK Bingo Headquarters.

4 and 1...Time for Fun

Boat Race
More Pimms anyone?

Once a year, a quarter of a million people with names like Sebastian, Ginny and His Lordship line a four mile stretch of the Thames to watch Oxford and Cambridge conduct a rowing race. And have a few drinks while they wait for anything interesting to happen.

In typical British fashion, both crews are known as 'blues', wear blue, and have a 'blue' boat, which is often yellow. Traditionally, the loser challenges the winner to a rematch so they can do it all over again the following year.

For the last 154 years, this exciting spectacle never ceases to amaze and surprise. Sometimes Cambridge beat Oxford. Sometimes Oxford beat Cambridge.

Another amazing surprise is how this event is still shown live on terrestrial television rather than pay-per-view Sky Box Office. Or at all. BBC handed over coverage to ITV in 2005 when it clashed with a repeat of *Dancing on Ice*.

Nevertheless, the Boat Race retains respectable TV viewing figures and further proof of the love Britain has for the event is its appearance at No.79 on Channel 4's '*100 Greatest Sporting Moments*', when the Cambridge boat sank.

Another contender, had Channel 4 cameras been around to film it, occurred in 1838. The Cambridge crew, trailing six lengths behind Oxford on the Surrey Bend, staged a mutiny when oarsman Bovington Seymour-Pierce was accused by his fellow 'blues' of the worst possible crime; deliberately splashing.

Seymour-Pierce was dropped off on a small uninhabited island due west of Hammersmith Bridge. Oxford went on to win by 598 lengths.

Bobbies

Good old-fashioned policing in good old-fashioned uniforms

The traditional beat bobby or 'copper' is a familiar sight on television shows such as *The Bill* and repeats of *Juliet Bravo* and *Dixon of Dock Green*. Catching robbers and telling small children the time aside, the role of the policeman has remained largely unaltered. One thing that has changed recently is an increase in the amount of paperwork, a bit like teachers but without the half-term holidays. Policemen in the UK have an awesome armoury at their disposal aimed at stopping baddies in their tracks and allowing our neighbourhoods to be safe. Deploying the half nelson or a clip round the ear are no match for most ne'r-do-wells, but top of the range in the policeman's arsenal is the truncheon. Whereas other police forces have tended to opt for a semi-automatic pistol, the British bobby can inflict a similarly swift and devastatingly effective blow to the legs with their wooden baton — equipment based on the morris dancer's stick but without the bells or ribbons.

Bowler Hats
Hats off to the bowler!

The bowler hat was the traditional headwear of the city gent.

The peak year for bowler hat sales was 1964, the same year Ian Fleming's *Goldfinger* hit UK movie screens starring Sean Connery as James Bond.

One of the evil hench men in the film was Odd Job, the baddie Goldfinger's Korean bodyguard, chauffeur, golf caddy and all round ruthless killer. Odd Job wore a rather stylish bowler hat…with a metal, razor-edged rim. When flung, frisbee style, the bowler hat could happily take somebody's head off. Whilst this 'optional extra' was never made available to the standard city gents' bowler, this was not a fact commonly known at the time. Hence the swift removal of a bowler hat, teamed with adopting the stance of a frisbee thrower would virtually guarantee a seat on the 7.23 to Waterloo.

Its decline in the 1970s is linked to the rise in popularity of the bobble hat.

The Odd Job Man

15

Bowls
A load of balls

Popular pastime for British old-timers. It's like marbles played on grass but the balls are bigger so players can see them.

British Institutions
There is nothing like a Dame

In a survey of Great British Institutions, Dame Vera Lynn was knocked off the top spot by Broadmoor Hospital. The Beatles were third.

British Summertime

Usually a Wednesday.

Caravans
Shed Dragging

Huge mobile motor homes (or Winnebagos) are a popular sight in parts of Europe, the US and Australia.

In Britain, however, these 30ft long vehicles, often themselves towing a small family hatchback, are shunned in favour of dragging a small shed on wheels behind a small family hatchback. To say caravans are a more popular sight on Britain's roads might be contested as 'slightly misleading' by the drivers and passengers in the average 74 car tail-back. But if it's 'slightly misleading' you're after, look no further than the names caravan manufacturers select in an effort to make these white plastic boxes seem a sensible alternative to going abroad:

Tornado
Swift
Concorde
Gulf Stream
Comet
Gazelle
Mirage
Mirage? If only!

Caravanners have adopted a siege mentality – a 'them' and 'us' approach – which they appear to revel in. They ignore the abuse and the blast of car horns with a polite doff of their flat caps and cheery 'v' sign. They stick those little multi-coloured plastic holiday destination flags to the rear window, much as a Spitfire pilot would mark his fuselage with enemy aircraft kills during World War II.

Whitby, Dartmoor, Lake District, Stonehenge, Ben Nevis all denote occupied territory during Bank Holidays and half-term.

In Britain, there is no road too small for the caravan – unlike their 30ft long cousin which would almost certainly take out three sets of traffic lights and a lamp post just trying to turn left out of the Winnebago showroom. The caravan has an access-all-areas pass and is relying only on the power of the car pulling it. And the driver. And the tow-bar not snapping off.

The versatile caravan is just as able to pootle down a country lane at 34mph as it is to pootle along the M1 at 34mph. In the slow lane. Then in the fast lane. Then back in the – no, wait a second – it's just wobbling.

Car Boot Sales
Like Antiques Roadshow... without the antiques

Car boot sales offer a tremendous opportunity to have a clear out and earn some cash at the same time. Any cash received in exchange for your valuable antiques and heirlooms (known in car boot parlance as 'old tat') is traditionally spent at the same event, purchasing other peoples' 'old tat' to fill the space recently created by having that clear out. A regular car boot event will feature up to 100 cars, one burger van and one Portaloo. The most common items for sale are:

1) Assorted VHS videos
2) Pub ashtrays
3) Foot spas
4) Car stereos
5) Cocktail shakers
6) Blue Peter Annuals

Carry On Films
'Oooh no, Matron...'

Nobody can do low budget comedy films like the British. The *Carry On* series was a fusion of low budget, double entendre, innuendo, farce and slapstick.

The 29 films released between 1958 and 1978 became classic British institutions. Amusingly, foreign visitors to Britain during that period were often disappointed to realise that the types of characters portrayed by the likes of Sid James, Kenneth Williams, Hattie Jacques and Charles Hawtrey, actually existed.

The 1969 release *Carry On Camping* features the most repeated film clip in televisual history; the outdoor aerobics scene. The scene launched aerobics into the UK and Babs's bikini top into an adjacent field.

Two of the leading stars went on to continue their TV careers with hilarious BBC sitcom *Terry and June*. Who can forget the side-splitting sketch involving the food processor spilling its contents onto Terry's suit? With laughs like these it was no surprise that *Terry and June* remained on our TV screens for nearly a decade, and on UKTV Gold ever since.

Commuting
Putting the 'rush' in crush

It's a well-known fact that workers in the UK put in more hours per week than all other European nations.

Country	Average Hours Worked (per Week)	Average commute to work
UK	42+	1 hour 47 minutes
Germany	40	54 minutes
Netherlands	31	15 minutes (via bicycle)
Belgium	29	45 minutes (via cake shop)
Italy	6.5	9 minutes (58 minutes if observing speed limits)

Commuting to work can create up to 35% more stress than the actual work itself.

When using public transport this figure rises slightly to 77%.

There are a number of unwritten rules that apply when using a train as part of a daily commute. The renewal of a monthly or weekly season ticket is left to the actual day of travel to ensure formation of an enormous and seething queue. Waiting for the train should take place at the exact same spot on the platform each morning and evening. This spot should not be marked in any visible way (i.e. by scuffing) to give any clues to a less experienced commuter.

If possible, when boarding the train, the same seat should be taken each morning. Should that seat already be occupied, a short sharp tut under one's breath, is permitted, before creating a huge kerfuffle in trying to find an empty seat. More commonly, there won't be a seat left in the first place, so standing in the aisle whilst trying to read a newspaper and hold onto something becomes the challenge.

Holding onto another commuter (seated or standing) is not recommended.

When leaving the train, allow enough time to push back through disembarking commuters to retrieve the umbrella you've left on the luggage rack. During peak times (6-9.30am and 4.30-8pm Monday-Friday), all normal rules of polite social behaviour are suspended.

Dog Lovers
Actually, its bite is worse than its bark

There's no better proof that the British are a nation of dog lovers than Crufts. This annual dog show, held at the NEC in Birmingham, attracts approximately 23,000 dogs and over 150,000 visitors. The Kennel Club admitted human error was to blame for a misunderstanding during the 2008 Gundog Group. The Best of Breed in the Flat Haired Retriever Group was originally awarded to *Northern Lights Superior Goldenmist Buccaneer Comet Masterpiece*, owned by a Mr. G Bullard of Penrith. *Northern Lights Superior Goldenmist Buccaneer Comet Masterpiece* was indeed owned by a Mr. G Bullard of Penrith. It was his 4 berth caravan, which was blocking the exit of the NEC car park.

Worse still, the dog looked like its owner

Driving on the Left
Mirror, signal, mano....swerve, swear, signal with fingers

Seventy-two per cent of the World drive on the right. Britain, together with Ireland, Cyprus and Malta are the only countries in Europe to do the exact opposite. Like a stubborn four-year-old.

An investigation into a sudden drop in the number of tourists visiting the UK has been linked to a dramatic increase in car accidents abroad.

The reduction in foreign visitors coincided with the release of a helpful Ministry of Transport factsheet aimed at visitors to the UK who were intending to drive:

'Visitors are informed that in the United Kingdom traffic drives on the left-hand side of the road. In the interests of safety you are advised to practise this in your country of origin before driving in the UK'.

The origins of driving on the left date back to the period when people believed the Earth was flat. By allowing vehicles to drive on the left, and then come back again on the right, most falling-off-the-edge related issues could be avoided.

31

Eccentrics
'Stand back madam, I'm an eccentric'

Since 1629, Britain has been producing more eccentrics per square mile than any other country.

According to the 37th *Debrett's Guide to Eccentrics* (with a foreword by HRH Prince Phillip) all the best eccentrics are either Lords, Earls or Dukes. Whilst being eccentric can often be mistaken for being completely bonkers, there is a big difference.

Pop songstrel Mariah Carey can produce a 22 page document on **exactly** what items should be provided for her backstage, but this behaviour is known as 'diva' (from the word 'div') rather than 'eccentric' behaviour.

A true eccentric would be called the Seventh Earl of Trowbridge, even when he wasn't. He would use a modified decommissioned submarine to attempt to break the world four-man bobsleigh record assisted by a launch mechanism designed from two deckchairs, a cricket bat and the parcel shelf from a 1926 Morris Bullnose.

Fish and Chips
Salt and vinegar?

The traditional British take-away has recently been replaced as the nation's favourite by a curry; however, mushy peas go better with fish and chips and a trip to 'the chippy' (also known in some regions as 'the fishy') is a weekly occurrence for most Brits. The practice of wrapping the fish and chips up in newspaper has been stopped after people began to believe one of the distinguishing features of the adult cod were the words 'England lose on penalties', just beneath the dorsal fins.

"One large cod please, mate"

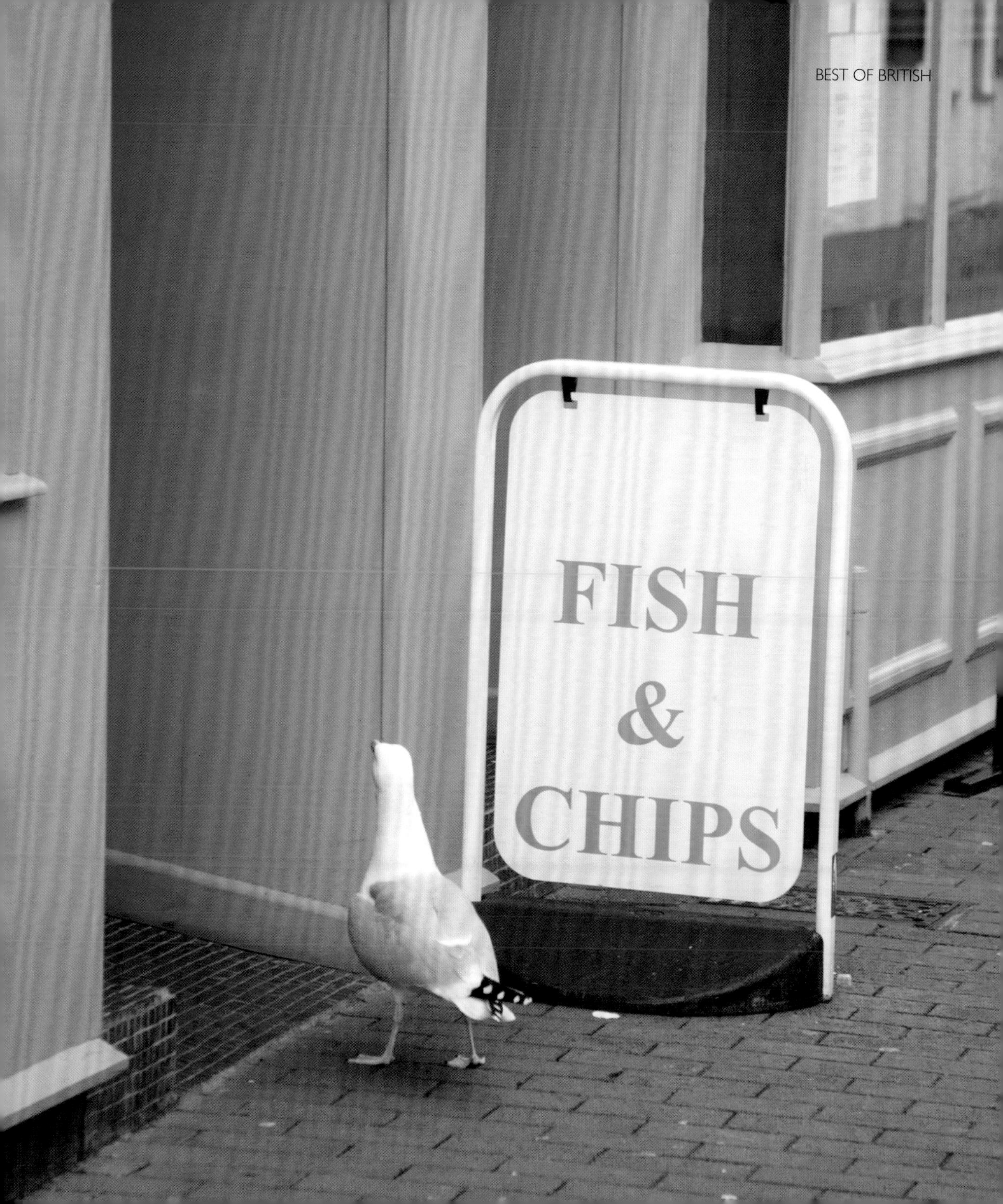
FISH
&
CHIPS

Flags
Flag sales flagging

One thing Britain hasn't quite got the hang of is proudly flying the national flag. To start with, there is a big debate over what the flag is even called. It could be a Union Flag or a Union Jack. Traditionally, a 'jack' was a flag flown on the bow of a boat but Parliament decided in 1908, after a particularly good lunch, that the national flag could be termed the Union Jack even if it was run up a flagpole on land. The Union flag/Jack is comprised of The Cross of St George, overlaid with St Patrick's cross (Ireland) and the saltire of St Andrew (Scotland). Whilst very clever, this design has proved virtually impossible for children and adults to draw accurately, hence it was decided not to even try and incorporate the Welsh dragon into the design. The Cross of St George on its own is seen slightly more than the Union Flag/Jack, on April 23rd, St Georges Day, or more usually when England are about to lose on penalties in a major football tournament.

During this period, most cars and vans on the roads of England will sport the cross of St George in a discreet manner. At all other times, this flag or the Union flag/Jack will rarely be seen in case it is perceived to be trading on past glories of the Empire – all seen as a bit big-headed and not very British.

Dorothy Tipsheet (72) from *Tipsheet's Flag and Bunting Emporium* believes it a great shame that every new home built in the UK doesn't have a flagpole in the garden. "I think they should be fitted as standard – like a kitchen or a roof" said Tipsheet.

"Saving your flags for best is all well and good but there just aren't enough Royal Weddings or Jubilee Years these days. Not like in the old days, when you could rely on England qualifying for a football tournament before losing to Germany on penalties – and back then you had the Home Internationals too".

*It was only when Jock and Hamish
looked in the mirror…*

Full English Breakfast
Greasing the spoons of the nation

The most important meal of the day is breakfast, so it naturally follows that it should set the standard in terms of health and nutrition.

Delivering a power-packed 485,683 calories, a 'Full English' (sometimes referred to as the 'Full Monty') blows Johnny Foreigner's continental breakfast of croissant, juice and a piece of fruit, clean out of the water. Britain cannot run on such lightweight sustenance and nothing can come close to that satisfied feeling from polishing off a Full English brekkers. Recent tests at Penzance University have shown that the 'satisfied feeling' is actually your arteries clogging up.

The main component parts of this 'proper' breakfast are: eggs, beans, grilled tomatoes, bacon, hash-browns (an introduction from the US – a bit like the grey squirrel, and only slightly tastier), fried bread, toast, black-pudding, sausages and lard.

The black pudding is an optional extra in more southerly parts of the UK but is supplied as standard in the North. It is made from pigs' blood, pork fat and either oatmeal or barley. If that sounds rather unappetising then it's probably safe to assume you should also avoid ordering haggis or Turkey Twizzlers.

Grand National
"And they're off...the jockeys have fallen off"

The annual horse racing event held at Aintree, Liverpool is rightly described as the 'World's Greatest Steeplechase'. Up to 600m people worldwide watch 40 of the best horses and jockeys navigate two stamina-draining circuits of the two and a quarter mile course. And to make it a little harder, 30 huge fences, ditches and water jumps have to be negotiated along the way. The potential for a horse to fall, pull up, be brought down, unseat the rider or many other potential hazards ensure that predicting the eventual outcome requires more than skill, judgement and a study of the form guide. As nearly half the population of the UK waging nearly £300m can confirm, other factors come into consideration; factors such as:

The significance of the draw…or sweepstake.

What colour will the jockeys be wearing? Do any of the names have a coincidental connection or significance? Is the jockey good-looking? Is there a grey horse that'll stand out on the telly? Should I use an actual pin or will any sharp pointy object do?

What's the least amount of money I can bet?

Great Britain
The clue is in the name

The British are generally a modest, unassuming bunch, but, beneath the façade is a steely determination, confidence and pride that helped make the country the current undisputed World War Champion of the World. Look again. There's a clue in the name United Kingdom of 'Great' Britain.

In 1997, 1999 and again in 2003, the French tried unsuccessfully to re-brand their country Great France. In 2005, Britain successfully copyrighted the name 'Great' ensuring that no other country could use the prefix.

However, the French are, by their very nature, not British and therefore unable to be gracious in defeat. High level discussions remain ongoing in Paris in an attempt to secure the rights to 'Even Greater'.

Guy Fawkes
Light blue touch paper and run

In 1605, Guy Fawkes and his fellow revolutionaries plotted to blow up King James I and the Houses of Parliament during the State Opening on November 5th. The codename for the operation was 'The Gunpowder Job'.

Fawkes, the explosives man, was captured shortly after he'd lit the blue touch paper that would have destroyed Protestant rule. The first fuse had fizzled out and the dilemma of knowing never to return to a lit firework was to be his undoing. Fawkes was hung, drawn and quartered; the penalty at the time for High Treason prior to ASBOs being introduced in 1988.

Today, Britain marks November 5th by selling fireworks to teenagers yet to already obtain an ASBO, from around September 3rd.

Bonfire Night events take place on those village greens that haven't been built on and provide *Blue Peter* with the opportunity to do a feature about hibernating hedgehogs.

Britain's most popular firework is the 'Mount Vesuvius: Flames of Fury' which takes its name from a popular dish at a Tandoori restaurant in Edgbaston. The Supa-Bomb Turbo Sky Burst can scare grannies and small animals from a distance of over seven miles. The Phoenix Mega-Stratosphere Bazooka Surprise is only available to qualified pyrotechnic event organisers and children returning from a school trip to France.

Knotted Handkerchief
Just apply sunburn

Britain has produced some of the best fashion designers in the world.

Paul Smith, Stella McCartney, Alexander McQueen and Vivienne Westwood have all identified a big summer trend *per homme* (for blokes) next season.

Already appearing on the catwalks of the Milan and Paris shows is the British fashion statement: the knotted handkerchief.

Fashionistas predict the trend next season will be to wear the hankerchief on top of a baldy head, at a slightly jaunty angle, and contrast the simple plain white cotton material with the vertical blue, red or green and white stripes of a deckchair. Each handkerchief or 'hankie' should be restricted to four simple double reef knots, tied in each corner.

Completing this bold summer look will involve falling asleep with mouth agape and in full sunshine.

"Ruddy seagulls!"

Milkman
Helping to wake up Britain every morning

Many Britons are still clinging to their morning delivery of milk, affectionately known as 'a pinta'.

Not so in Europe, where the metric system has overrun the imperial system in much the same way as the British native red squirrel has been run out of town by the North American Grey Squirrel interloper.

Meanwhile, back on British milkmen, the advantages of having your daily 'pinta' delivered at 4.30am or possibly 11.30am, or anytime in between, enormous.

For a start, you don't have to go to the corner shop or supermarket ever again.

Well, maybe you do, but not for milk, allright?

And why pay supermarket prices when you can pay a bit more? There's no doubt that you can taste the difference between milks, but only if one has been left on your doorstep in the sun for about four hours and been attacked by blue tits. Otherwise, it's all just milk.

The milkman's company vehicle, or float, is designed to silently glide from street to street in an economic, quiet and environmentally friendly fashion. Powered by fourteen 'AAA' long lasting rechargeable

The innovative location of the T400i windscreen wiper is a
result of the windscreen being fitted upside down

batteries and some big cogs, the designs for the milkfloats of today have come a
long way.

According to *WhatFloat?* magazine, the latest top of the range Hemmingford
T400i 'Whisper' has satellite navigation, cruise control and paperboy sensors fitted
as standard. With a range of seven miles on a full charge, the T400i 'Whisper' is
effortlessly able to overtake caravans, boasts a 0-3mph in 38 seconds and can
carry 12,000 pints of milk – enough to wake up the whole neighbourhood. The
'Whisper LX' has an optional roofrack for sliced bread and yoghurts.

Morris Dancers
Dancing with bells on

The origins of grown men with beards attaching bells to their cricket whites and heading off to the nearest pub for a dance with a wooden stick is somewhat shrouded in mystery. Suffice to say, it's a tradition that is yet to take Continental Europe by storm. Recent studies suggest that it dates back to a group of Morris Minor motor car enthusiasts and rival supporters who preferred the sportier Austin Seven.

To decide which was indeed the best British car, the Morris supporters challenged the Austin supporters to a dance-off at their local hostelry over the Bank Holiday weekend. Fuelled by industrial quantities of real ale, the two teams battled it out in a series of increasingly complicated choreographed moves and occasional whooping noises. With the Morris men deemed the winners, they went on to challenge all-comers, seeing off supporters of the Triumph Herald, Austin Maestro, Vauxhall Victor and Rover 2000 in the space of six months.

But there may be another explanation.

Chorus: "Four cylinders, overhead valve, eight hundred and three cc, the Morris Minor is the only car for me."

Museums
Do not touch the glass

Britain has the largest amount of museums per capita in the world.

The British Museum, The Natural History Museum, Doncaster Bobble Hat Museum, Dalkeith's interactive Marbles Museum and Garden Spade World in Cardiff all jostle to attract their share of visitors. One thing they all share in common is over-priced gift shops selling cuddly toys loosely based on the theme of the museum. And an enormous entrance fee.

Mushy Peas
Simply the mushiest

A mainstay of British cuisine is mushy peas. Whilst black pudding or haggis make an effort to disguise what they really are, mushy peas have no need for such a clumsy smokescreen. There's just no getting around the fact that mushy peas are just that. So build a bridge and get over it.

Often seen as just an accompaniment to fish and chips, it is a big mistake to think that this versatile pea-based dish does not have a few serving suggestions of its own. There are, in fact, numerous regional variations for the unfeasibly bright green foodstuff. One from the Derbyshire area is mushy peas and chips. So, like fish and chips but without the fish part. Another dish, popular in Yorkshire and Nottinghamshire, involves having the mushy peas but not with the fish or the chips.

In some parts of Britain, and especially popular with students returning from the pub with the munchies, mushy peas are eaten as a late night snack with a couple of fried eggs and a pork pie. Or whatever else hasn't gone two months over the 'best before' date.

Panic Buying

The British can panic buy like no other nation. The best time to witness this shopping technique used to be in the run up to Christmas. The combination of the imminent arrival of relatives, coupled with the fact that supermarkets will be shut for one day is an itch that demands to be scratched.

Hence, shoppers end up purchasing a huge array of 'seasonal foodstuffs' such as festive pickles and chutneys, destined to remain unopened until the following Christmas. And why just buy one packet of Eat Me Dates when, if you buy three, the fourth box is free?

In recent years, panic buying has become more widespread, causing even greater panic.

For example, the merest hint of industrial action at a UK oil terminal never used to receive coverage on the national news. For starters, any strike or threatened closure would invariably get called off 24 hours before it was due to start anyway. Besides, around two months' worth of petrol and diesel reserves exist to cover any such eventuality. So they say.

These days, media channels justify that the possibility of strike action is a public service announcement because it's important everybody realises that there is absolutely no need, reason or justification to 'panic buy'.

Ten minutes later, queues start forming at every petrol station. And those reserves that would *normally* last two months…

A more sensible public broadcast would be to announce that there is no need to panic buy Eat Me Dates in the run up to this Christmas because there are already unopened reserves lasting 10 years in most kitchens across Britain.

Pantomime
"It's behind you!"

The pantomime is a great and unique British tradition (one that is impossible to explain to Americans) providing a fabulous opportunity to hoot with laughter, forget all your troubles and loudly shout 'Who?!'

A poster advertising a forthcoming pantomime is guaranteed to cheer up even the most miserable soul. Study without a flicker of recognition the 'star-studded' cast and then look for the explanation in brackets underneath e.g. "The one on crutches in TV's *Holby City* Radio 207.6fm's traffic girl" and "PC Gary Wilson in Channel 5's police drama that clashes with *EastEnders*".

A glittering TV and showbiz career?
It's behind you!

Hours of fun for all the family.

"…and this year, to avoid any repeat of Gordon Hopwood's unfortunate straddling incident, we've lowered the seventeenth fence"

Patron Saints
Situations vacant

The UK has four Patron Saints. Due to exciting expansion plans, applications are now invited for the newly created position of Patron Sinner. This is a busy and demanding role and the ideal candidate must be dynamic, flexible and extremely well-organised, demonstrating the ability to manage a highly varied workload. A creative flair would be an advantage. This exceptional opportunity offers full training, attractive salary package and benefits.

The Patron Saint of England is St George (April 23rd). Every year, the English half-heartedly make a claim for a public holiday even though nobody really celebrates apart from running gag Dorothy Tipsheet (72) and a few morris dancers. And besides, the date tends to be midweek and clashes with something good on the telly.

The Patron Saint of Scotland is St Andrew. Celebrated on November 30th the day is marked by the traditional turning on of the central heating.

On March 1st, Wales celebrates St David's Day, which is traditionally a day of taking the dog for a slightly longer walk and maybe watching a DVD later.

On March 17th all hell breaks lose. It's St Patrick's Day and a public holiday in Northern Ireland, which is such a great 'craic' the rest of the UK gatecrashes. It's a day of curly green wigs, Guinness and of everybody wishing they had a Patron Saint like Paddy.

Personal Space

Researchers at Liverpool's John Lennon University have been studying the accepted minimum distance between two strangers. In their landmark *Sociological & Behavioural Studies* paper entitled 'What Personal Space Is', they concluded there are two main categories. The first, used to describe an acceptable distance to create an ambience conducive to social interaction, they named as 'comfortable'. The second describes 'that edgy feeling you get when somebody you don't really know stands too close'. The latter scenario was labelled by the researchers as 'uncomfortable'. The researchers then conducted a benchmark five year study across various sunny parts of Europe to establish if there was any difference in 'personal space parameters' between European nations.

Summarising the 27 pages of untidy writing covered in suncream marks and an enclosed flyer advertising the Club Fantasia @ Playa del Sol (first drinks free) didn't take very long. In conclusion, getting within three feet of a British individual who doesn't know you, is likely to cause an effect identified as an 'invasion of personal space'.

Picnics (see also lay-bys)
Enjoying the 'Great British Outdoors'

The tradition of a summer picnic dates back to before *Coronation Street* began.

With military-style planning, beginning with a dawn raid on the nearest 24 hour supermarket, the picnic is the British response to continental Europe's extravagant claims to outdoor living.

Emptying the supermarket shelves of bread, tomatoes, ham, crisps, sausage rolls, pork pies, scotch eggs, apples and fizzy drinks is just for starters. Loading up the assembled picnic into a large blue coolbox and the family into the family car is a business that requires around two hours longer than planned. Also shoe-horned into the car boot will be deckchairs, frisbee, swingball, blankets (for sitting on…or huddling beneath), sunshades or umbrella, cricket set, thermos flasks of tea or coffee and multi-coloured stripy windbreak. The more ambitious picnic may also involve a disposable barbecue. Invariably, nobody will bring any matches.

Following an average 3 hour 45 minute drive (not including toilet breaks) the 17-mile journey will culminate in the arrival at the predetermined 'nice spot'. After queuing for a further hour to get into the car park, the picnic can begin!

Firstly, a car door or boot must be left open and all the windows are lowered about three centimetres. The picnic is then removed and placed on a blanket spread on the grass in the car park, immediately next to the vehicle from whence it came.

So as not to intrude on the family doing exactly the same thing, three feet to the right, the wind break is used as a temporary boundary.

Enjoying 'The Great Outdoors' and a pork pie at exhaust pipe level, watching more and more cars try and find less space may not be everybody's thermos flask of tea. Therefore the 'beauty spot' may also contain the slightly less adventurous (or 'older') picnicker who, tired out from the drive and from trying to keep wasps off their sandwiches, will be sitting in their car enjoying Radio 4. The doors, windows and eyelids all firmly shut…the mouth, wide open, like a basking shark filtering plankton.

Post boxes
Pillars of society

There are approximately 110,000 traditional pillar box red post boxes in the UK.

Of these, 53 are emptied regularly (except Sundays and Bank Holidays).

The iconic British post box, originated some 150 years ago when letters must have been really, really small. Recently an English Heritage campaign to preserve the remaining boxes was announced. The aim is to protect and restore the three different existing types of traditional red boxes and to ensure the cast iron structures with a small slot at the top for your letters, cannot be demolished without planning permission and a JCB. Mind you, they said the same about red telephone boxes.

Interestingly, a quick glance at a well known internet trading website reveals a number of post boxes currently for sale. One seller, also offering a JCB digger for hire, has an original cast iron ER II pillar box for sale at £2,400 (plus £95 postage).

Quite how a post box will fit inside another post box remains to be seen, but it could be a long awaited British rival to those Russian Babushka dolls. Or it could be long awaited like the second class post.

The Proms
A bastion of Britishness

The *Last Night of the Proms* with its colourful chorus of 'Land of Hope and Glory' is universally accepted as an evening to boost a shared cultural identity and make the British feel massively proud to be…British.

The Prime Minister regards the Proms as a "bastion of Britishness". Nobody quite knows what he means but it's a phrase also used for Wimbledon, Royal Ascot, HP Sauce and a new shopping centre in Coventry.

Dorothy Tipsheet (72) from *Tipsheet's Flag and Bunting Emporium* regards the annual event as vital to her business.

"It's vital, dear" said a sprightly Tipsheet, "yet what people don't realise is that I sell twice as much bunting to the local residents celebrating the fact that it's over. All those people coming to town for the Proms means they can't park their cars in their drives you see, and having to listen to that dreadful racket. Now **they** really celebrate the last night of the Proms, they do".

Pubs
Alcoholic beverage emporiums

The traditional second home of most Brits is the public house or 'the local'.

According to research, a pub will provide a huge range of alcoholic beverages and intoxicating liquors to anybody over the age of 18, in an environment that provides all the comforts of your own front room, but with a larger telly and a load of strangers.

Providing fruit machines, a juke box, pub quizzes and a three-day old copy of *The Sun* is fairly standard, as is an intriguing array of real ale with names like *Auld Fursty Badger, Ramsbottom Goldenferret Wizardsnake* and *Champion Thoroughbred Marriage Wrecker.*

Real ales are very potent and often served in rusty, slightly dented tankards to rusty, slightly dented drinkers. Unreal ales are best avoided.

Pub quizzes have become a popular method of attracting customers to the hostelry and each group must provide their own amusing team name such as *Auld Fursty Badger, Ramsbottom Goldferret Wizardsnake* or *The Know It-Ales.*

Darts and dominoes are provided to cater for the sporty, whilst catering elsewhere is usually in the form of assorted bar snacks aimed at helping customers try and soak up their drinks rather than the atmosphere.

It is safe to say that the British and pubs go together like a coach and horses; to imagine life without a local would be like a dog without a duck.

Punch and Judy
Not to be confused with Richard and Judy

A traditional sight in British seaside resorts is a red and white stripy tent with a man in it.

He's just changing into his trunks probably, but not far away, in another red and white stripy tent, there's the Punch and Judy man. This puppet show theatre, dating back to the sixteenth century, features the sort of violence that is usually only witnessed on episodes of *The Simpsons*.

The characters include Mr Punch, Judy his wife, a baby, a crocodile, a policeman and the devil. And a string of sausages. The plot is a bit vague, not helped by the fact that Mr Punch has a silly voice, like he's on helium, but small children don't seem to mind a bit and will sit cross-legged, happily shouting abuse for hours whilst their parents desperately search the beach looking for them.

"Hey, you're not the Punch and Judy man"

Queen's English
'How now brown cow innit'

The Queen's English or upper received pronunciation is now only spoken by Her Majesty and some of her friends. Estuary English has become the most common form of pronunciation, though its similarities with the Cockney dialect have made the borders increasingly blurred. Use of the word 'never' (e.g. 'he never did') and characteristic pronunciation of the words 'water', 'grass' and 'bath' followed by the word 'innit' would usually suggest *EastEnders* has just started.

Queueing
We love it!

The absolute giveaway to British national identity is the ability to form an orderly queue with just two people.

Queue-jumping is still regarded by English Civil Law to be punishable by death, though this has rarely been enforced for some reason.

The British will naturally form an orderly queue, referred to as a 'line' in the US and a waste of time everywhere else. Bizarrely, the attitude of patiently awaiting one's turn by queuing has been discontinued on the Nations road network. In recent years it has become an accepted rule of driving on Britain's roads that queuing is for everybody else.

Semi-professional queueing involves camping out, and is best witnessed in December for the forthcoming January sales or for returning unwanted Christmas presents. Other queuing hotspots are anywhere in Heathrow Terminal 5 and grannies trying to get front-row tickets for a Cliff Richard concert. These queues can last for weeks and are virtually guaranteed local or national TV coverage.

Some of the longest recorded queues in the UK are as follows:
WHSmith Sheffield– 0.75 miles (new Harry Potter book)
New NHS Dentist, Dundee – 8 miles
Heathrow Terminal Five 2008 (opening day of new state-of-the-art check-in system) – 8.5 miles

Ramblers
Turning walking into a sport

If the game of golf is 'a good walk ruined' then ramblers can ruin your game of golf by unexpectedly trooping across the fairway just as you're about to play a tricky par four.

Britain has more ramblers than any other country, making it a big business opportunity for retail outlets catering specifically for their needs. By clever marketing techniques, a simple walk in the country now requires 48kg of 'specialist' equipment costing an average £986.82.

Bright orange anoraks (breathable element defence systems) designed specifically to clash with all other colours known to man, are worn over four other waterproof layers and a fleece. Large square, clear plastic map covers with loops for around the neck are teamed with expensive, hand-held, GPS satellite navigation systems. Each rambler, or more often, group of around 25 ramblers, must each carry an enormous rucksack containing spare socks, water bottle, torch, Kendal mint cake, lightweight waterproof trousers (khaki or beige), and ironing board.

The absolute 'must have' for the semi-professional rambler has become the high tension anti-shock walking poles made from aircraft grade aluminium and featuring tungsten tips.

To avoid one of these tungsten tips connecting with your buttocks it is strongly advised that upon seeing ramblers with walking poles on a warm summer day, that you do not start loudly humming the theme music to BBC TV's *Ski Sunday*.

Red Squirrel
Squirrel Wars: The Phantom Menace

One of the most charming species of small mammals in Britain is the red squirrel, the only squirrel native to Britain. It was doing just fine, thanks, until somebody decided one type of squirrel in Britain wasn't enough and introduced the grey squirrel in 1876. The grey squirrel (Horridus rattis) has thrived and red squirrel numbers declined. What is most disappointing is that the greys just nick the nuts from your bird feeder.

Tufty reluctantly accepted that his nut stash had been concreted over for 'an outstanding new development of two, three and four bedroom homes'

Sense of Fair Play
Or making losing acceptable

No matter what the occasion, the British are always top of the imaginary Fair Play League.

The committee behind spending three times its budget for the 2012 Olympics is trying to introduce 'fair play' as a sport (together with darts and fishing), in the hope of Britain getting a bronze medal in something. Competitors in Team GB will have 'It's not the winning – it's the taking part' embroidered on their tracksuits (beside that splodge that looks like they've spilt something but on closer inspection is actually the official 2012 logo).

It's a phrase that will be familiar to anybody who has ever watched the Eurovision Song Contest.

The fact remains, the British actually want to win more than anybody else, and when this doesn't happen, an in-built sense of fair play comes to the fore. This is to be expected from a civilised nation that invented cricket, the only sport to feature a drinks trolley.

If the British can't win then victory can still be sought on the moral high ground – the territory of 'fair play'. Being 'plucky' or 'gallant' in defeat (words closely associated with Wimbledon fortnight) is a bit like a skill and is far superior to being a big fat Johnny Show Off.

'Jolly well played Fritz, I didn't think you'd save my penalty'

In competition, the British shun the very notion of being over-confident and all the added pressure that is associated with expectation. As a result, the British have become champion underdogs.

The underdog was a close second behind the Yorkshire Terrier in a 'Best of British' survey at Crufts last year.

Socks and Sandals
Wrong on every level

Sandals for blokes are known as 'mandals'. Teaming socks with mandals is a fashion trend believed to have originated in the Basingstoke area.

During the long hot summer of 1976, as temperatures soared to above 70 degrees, civil servants at Hampshire County Council voted by committee, two steering panels, a referendum, a pre-meeting, a long lunch and three summit meetings that it was too hot to wear stout black lace-ups.

This classic British look is referred to in hushed tones of reverence within French fashion circles as a 'faux-pas'.

Stiff Upper Lip
Triumphing in the face of adversity

The British triumph in the face of adversity. They thrive on it – positively encouraging adversity to strike by antagonising it with a sharp and pointy stick. And then laughing.

According to dusty old journals behind a radiator in The British Library, the British individual officially acknowledged as possessing the stiffest upper lip was intrepid 1920s' jungle explorer Colonel Jeremy Trousers-Downe.

Having faced years of hard knocks and teasing for being named Jeremy, Trousers-Downe had developed a thick skin, just above his top lip.

Whilst exploring in the Amazon jungle in 1924, he was captured by hostile spear-waving tribesmen after his canoe had capsized into piranha infested waters. As the Colonel was being lowered into a large flaming cauldron, he declared "Marvellous…that'll dry my trousers off nicely" before asking his captors for the latest score in the Test Match.

Small Talk
Breaking those uncomfortable silences

When it comes to making 'small talk' there's only one topic of conversation for the British. For any situation urgently demanding the need to break an uncomfortable silence with some small talk, the default topic is the weather.

Interestingly, this is not the case in Europe, where similar circumstances are met head-on with a variety of non-meteorological themed subjects.

A major EU study in Brussels revealed that the number one subject for small talk in France concerns the current price of cheese. The Danish would invariably open a conversation by voicing an opinion on their national entry in the Eurovision Song Contest, whilst the Italians would discuss the current week's Government.

Most other countries surveyed found small talk was actually in decline, and has been replaced with a silent stare, combined with a quizzically raised eyebrow.

Small talk. Big phone bill.

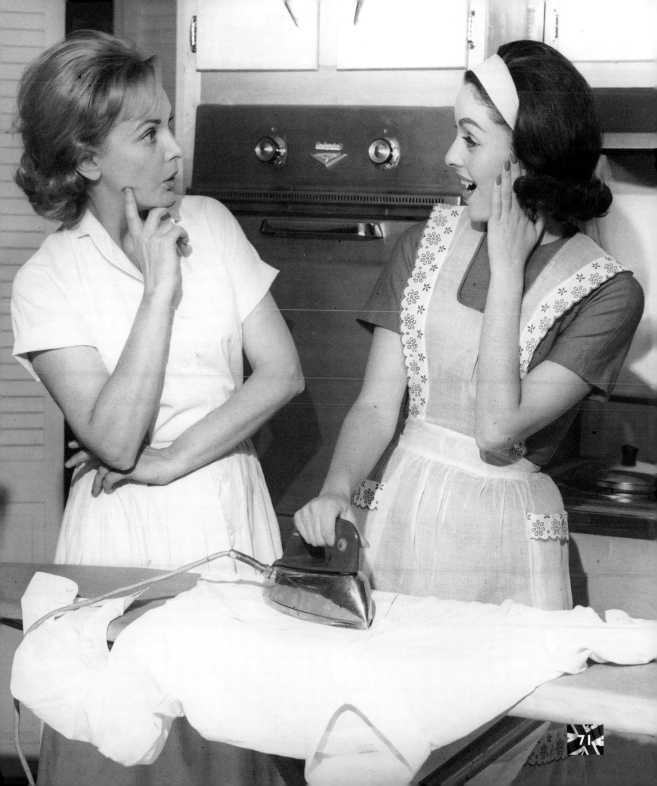

Sunday Roast
Meat and two veg

The traditional British Sunday lunch is the 'Roasty'. The most popular combination is a joint of roast beef with Yorkshire pudding. Roast pork with stuffing and apple sauce, roast lamb with mint sauce or roast chicken or duck are equally popular alternatives to British non-vegetarians.

The roast meat dish is served with a selection of vegetables known collectively as 'all the trimmings'. This usually refers to a tasty combination of roasted potatoes, carrots, cabbage, swede, parsnips, peas and runner beans. Home-grown vegetables, or those sourced from an allotment rather than a supermarket, should be covered particularly generously in the gravy provided.

The furthest distance travelled on a regular basis for a Sunday roast is 275 miles, from Warwickshire to the Isle of Wight. A 74-year-old man has been making the journey for over 25 years; fleeing his wife's cooking in favour of a Hampshire pub and clocking up enough miles to have driven seven times around the World in the process. Regularly leaving at 6am each Sunday morning, he returns around noon the following Monday – a scene that will probably strike a chord with more women than you might imagine.

Noticing his side plate, Edward instantly regretted asking for 'all the trimmings' the day after he'd cut the hedge

Taxis
"Are you sure this is a short cut?"

The traditional London black cab, like the London double-decker bus is a British icon.

To become a licensed taxi driver in London a driver must study and pass 'The Knowledge'. The cab driver must establish a detailed knowledge of all the streets and places of interest in addition to displaying a general knowledge of the major arterial routes in the capital. Learning 'The Knowledge' takes an average of four years to become an 'all-London' cab driver and is tested by Public Carriage Office examiners.

This test differs slightly from that of some continental countries. Would-be taxi drivers overseas must demonstrate an ability to drive whilst simultaneously making wild hand gestures and whistling loudly at attractive female pedestrians.

Tea
"Put the kettle on, love"

Britain is a nation of tea drinkers. Walk down any high street and you'll almost certainly find a Costa Coffee, Starbucks Coffee, Coffee Republic or Café Nero which, er, proves it.

What is essentially a very simple hot beverage can actually be made to an infinite amount of combinations using different types of tea to determine the strength and taste. Sugar and milk are both optional.

Earl Grey, English Breakfast and Assam are just three I can think of right now, but there are more varieties. Having a cream tea (with optional scone) combined with a nice sit down, is a sure-fire way of solving most problems; from world peace and global warming to which shoes to wear tonight.

The biggest debating point is whether one should put the milk in before the water, or after?

Betty Olde of 'The Olde Tea Shoppe' in York explains that the perfect brew, "should introduce the milk to the cup first dear", before then chattering on at considerable length about 'one for the pot', a knitted tea cosy her Aunt made and what nice weather we've been having.

A massive 80% of British office workers claim they find out more about what's going on over a cup of tea than in any other way; however, quite how beneficial to British business it is learning that Kerry in Accounts fancies the new post room guy remains somewhat questionable.

Tassology, the art of reading tea leaves (even using a tea bag) can help people believe aspects of their life are represented by the shape and position of tea leaves in a teacup.

For example, if the tea residue is in the form of a mushroom, this indicates an upcoming temporary or permanent move. If the tea is in the shape of a squirrel, this is a sign you should start saving some money.

Kayleigh-Jo Price (23) of Lincoln has no doubts about the accuracy of the messages from her regular workplace cuppa. She recalls "I was working at a local Estate Agent when I got into tassology - I'd be having about 43 tea-breaks a day. Anyway, I'll never forget the brew where I got a mushroom and squirrel shape – clear as anything they were! Then, about half an hour later, I was coming back off my tea break and I got sacked".

The Great British Reserve
We're famous for it - we just don't like to shout about it

Non-UK residents should be aware that The Great British Reserve takes a well-earned break during the January Sales or when the auditions for the 'X' Factor are taking place.

A different Great British Reserve can be found on the edge of the Dale peninsula in Pembrokeshire – a 35 acre tranquil haven for badgers, otters and of course squirrels.

Another example of a Great British reserve is for a table for two at 8pm

These examples should not be confused with Strawberry jam, a Great British Preserve.

When she ignored his offer of a handshake, Douglas felt well outside his comfort zone

77

Tipping
What's the minimum amount acceptable?

British people love rules. Whether they choose to obey them is an entirely different matter. As there are no firm ground rules for tipping, it is little wonder that waiters and waitresses across the world are often bemused by the small collection of coins and pocket fluff, left by the side of a bill by the British tourist.

Service included? Service not included? If it's not included is it not obligatory? Or is that a double negative? A double negative sounds about right as they were rather slow taking our order. And they didn't seem to see the funny side when Uncle Barry fell off his chair laughing after our kid threw up. And they never do chips like we get at home. If we tip the restaurant, should we tip the taxi home? He's just doing his job after all. They both are. And, rather than waste it, I can use the change for the fruit machine at the resort's traditional Irish pub.

Train Spotting
The popular hobby for 'men of a certain age'

The hobby of train-spotting has evolved greatly over the past 75 years. Originally the pastime of small boys in short trousers, who would peer over a local railway bridge to collect the names of the locomotives, waving happily as they thundered past, steam bellowing and whistle blowing. All through the lazy days of those golden summer holidays, knapsacks contained a packed lunch and lemonade nearby; pedal bicycles were abandoned haphazardly on the grassy verge.

The pastime has now become the almost exclusive occupation for men-of-a-certain-age in anoraks (but still those short trousers), who gather at the far end of station platforms such as Clapham Junction, Crewe and Cardiff Central. To distinguish train-spotters from the far more common hapless commuter desperately awaiting a glimpse of their train, an EU Directive from Brussels has suggested a re-branding to 'Train Bothering'.

Tutting
The failsafe technique for dealing with all unsatisfactory situations

One of the downsides of 'The Great British Reserve' is not being able to cause a big scene. Shouting and swearing enthusiastically whilst waving your arms about and making hand gestures is best left to the experts – the Italians.

Whilst the English language provides an enormous choice of colourful metaphors to use in 'unsatisfactory situations', the automatic application of the Great British Reserve ensures a mark of such displeasure is often restricted and condensed to a simple 'tut'.

Overcoming this, the British have developed a rather sophisticated 'sub-language' of tuts and sighs applied at varying degrees of volume.

Imagine the everyday scenario, waiting patiently in line for an available cashier at the Post Office, whereupon one has the misfortune to come across what is commonly known as a 'queue-jumping chancer'.

In such a situation the loud 'tut and sigh combo' although towards the top end of the scale, should be the tut of choice.

Watching somebody pull into the 'ten items or less' checkout with an overflowing trolley would warrant the same…unless it was a genuine mistake; in which case a 'treble tut and head-shake' should be employed.

Hearing your train is delayed half an hour due to 'wet leaves on the line' or 'the wrong kind of snow' is worthy of a single short, sharp tut of maximum volume.

In St Albans, locals fondly recollect Arthur Frobisher a retired town planner and general nuisance, who developed such a sophisticated range of tuts and sighs that he phased out using the English language completely.

Umbrellas
'It was a black one...'

The UK is the leading global market for umbrellas. Shares in the umbrella related manufacturing industry reached an all-time high this summer with fourteen companies quoted in the London FT Stock Exchange. Shares in *World of Rain PLC* rose 42.5p on news that the long range weather forecast predicted a dry spell. Meanwhile, shares in *Brollylolly* hardened at 471¾ on rumours of a takeover with French bleu-chip *Parasolaire*. Trading was suspended for two hours whilst City analysts tried to prevent umbrella shares going up the drainpipe down and down the drainpipe up.

The multi-million pound umbrella industry spends an average £16 per annum on research and development. This is £4 less than the average UK spend (per head) on replacing umbrellas that have been blown inside out following a light gust of wind or a sneeze.

According to Public Transport figures, approximately 450,000 umbrellas are left on Britain's buses and trains each year, mainly during June and July.

Whilst nearly all are recovered and handed in to Lost Property offices, they are rarely reunited with their owners. Lost Property staff hoping to retrieve the forgotten item seek a slightly more accurate description than, "It was a black one".

Today will be bright with warm sunny spells,
top temperature 28°C (83°F)…

Village Green
Acquired for development

One of the quintessential British scenes is that of the village green.

A common sight on a green is a game of cricket. A common sight on a common is a big dog doing its business by the swings.

Currently, the traditional village green is under threat since all the school playing fields have been built on. Look out for new two, three and four bedroom housing developments with ironic names such as 'Village Green Acres', 'Cricket Field Mews' and 'The Boundaries'.

Weather (Drought)
Forecasting a hosepipe ban

A drought is only officially recognised by the London Weather Centre in the event that precise meteorological patterns occur. Such conditions are determined with reference to the status defined by the UK industry standard *Meteorological Drought Alert Barometer.* ®™

According to the exacting circumstances specified, appropriate measures and restrictions can be imposed by local Government authorities.

Amber Alert: (Three consecutive sunny days) leading to:

- Hosepipe ban
- Bath-sharing advisory
- Photos of girls on beach appear in newspapers

Flashing Amber Alert: (Four consecutive sunny days) leading to:

- Re-launch of 'Use Water Wisely' campaign in press and media
- Ban on more than two cups of tea per day
- Photos of girls on different beach appear in newspapers
- Road and rail chaos due to 'extreme weather'

Red Alert: Official Drought (Five days of nice sunshine with the 'warm spell set to continue for the weekend'. Excludes Bank Holidays)

- Increases in barbecue-related injuries and water rates
- Photos of dried up reservoirs appear in media
- Underneath much larger picture of girl in a bikini enjoying an ice cream
- Annoying bloke at work greets everybody with 'hot enough for you?'

Flood Alert: Two consecutive days of rain – with possibility for more

- Increased demand for sandbags
- Road and rail chaos due to 'extreme weather'
- Re-launch of 'Is Your Journey Really Necessary' campaign in press and media
- Photos in papers of vehicles stranded in floodwater
- Good spot for catching mackerel

Weather (Forecasters)
Forecasting can be inaccurate due to unforeseen circumstances

"Earlier on today apparently a lady rang the BBC and said she heard that there was a hurricane on the way. Well, don't worry if you're watching, there isn't."

So said BBC weatherman Michael Fish on the evening before the Great Storm of 1987. And how right he was. Sure, the storm took out 15 million trees and cost an estimated £18bn to clear up. But it wasn't a hurricane. Oh no.

An unofficial Met Office spokesperson recalls; "A hurricane is a term used for a storm that develops in the tropics. This storm started as an area of low pressure in The Bay of Biscay. So it wasn't. And anyway, Uncle Michael forecasted it. On 15th October the depression suddenly began heading towards the UK, deepening to a pressure of 964mb by tea time. I remember there was lots of excited chat at the Met Office about 'back-pedalling over the horizon' so I knew something big was going down. By 10.30 that evening, winds of Force 10 were correctly and accurately noticed as the depression tracked across Southern England, at exactly which time we forecasted it with 100% accuracy. And for it to be a hurricane you need sustained winds of 73 mph or more. On this particular occasion, winds measured 120mph… but we don't count *gusts*. We switch to converting wind speed to knots if it looks like we've made a boo-boo."

To avoid weathermen becoming scapegoats, the BBC now operates a 'squad rotation system'; an initiative borrowed from some of the top football clubs in The Premiership. Drawing from a selection of 48 forecasters, it is now unusual to see the same presenter on TV for more than two days running without being rotated for an alternative presenter. 'Squad' forecasters may be given an opportunity on BBC 4 or BBC News 24, working up to the ultimate stage and flagship show: the Nine o'Clock News on BBC 1.

Weather (Long Range Forecasts)
As useful as long range shoe polish

The attraction of the UK long-range forecast is that by the time the period concerned arrives, everybody has forgotten what the forecast was. These 'seasonal' forecasts, introduced in Britain in 1992, are of particular appeal when forecasting the following 24 hours is proving a bit tricky. For reasons not quite fully understood, a long-range 'special' in early March for the summer ahead is regarded as totally believable, despite the forecast given on a Tuesday, for Wednesday morning, proving to be utter, utter rubbish.

White Van Man
On a Friday afternoon, three blokes in a Transit can outpace a Ferrari 440

The phenomenon known as 'White Van Man' has its origins in the UK.

The first recorded incidence, identifying this dangerously aggressive sector of the motoring public, was by Prof. Gordon Monkfish at Anglesey University in 1974.

Prof. Monkfish was studying the decline in numbers of the Great Crested Newt; one of the UK's protected species, when his research vehicle was cut up outrageously by a white Ford Transit van travelling at high speed. Concluding that the local newt population had probably had it, he began to study white vans instead.

His landmark research can be viewed at Anglesey University library, where it remains in use to this day since was written in red felt-tip pen on the inside front cover of *A Beginner's Guide to Newts and other Amphibians*.

By numbering the road cones marking a lane closure from 1-100, Monkfish established that the white van driver would, on average, aim for cone number 87 before contemplating changing lane, cone number 93 before reducing speed and cone number 97 before indicating.

Monkfish also concluded that the likelihood of being cut up by a white van was increased by a factor of seven should there be any football on the telly.

At the time of writing, the vehicle with the most unpaid parking tickets is a white Ford Transit van, with outstanding fines totalling an astonishing £42,000 from 264 tickets.

Wimbledon
"Anyone for tennis?"

The All England Lawn Tennis and Croquet Club provides a glorious fortnight of the British moaning about the weather, the price of strawberries and consistent inability to produce tennis players that can get beyond the first round.

In recent years, because the traditional June and July weather has delayed matters, the rest day or 'middle Sunday' has been used to play catch up. Britain has produced some of the best catch-up players in the world but hasn't produced a Wimbledon tennis champion for over 30 years. The middle Sunday becomes known as the 'People's Sunday' and is often when British pop legend Sir Cliff Richard gives an impromptu solo performance to the rain-lashed and rapidly emptying courts. If this continues to the second Sunday, it carries over to the Monday 'Monday Final' at which point All England officials thank Cliff very much but suggest he makes this his last song.

The main Centre Court opened around 1922 but queues had been forming from before six o'clock the previous day.

It remains the only Grand Slam tournament to enforce a dress code of 'almost entirely white', a rule dating back to original All England member and mixed doubles champion* Retd. Major Persil 'Daz' Doorstep-Challenge.

The prize money for the Wimbledon Gentlemen's and Ladies' finalists was traditionally wildly different, with the men walking away with a cool £500,000 and the women receiving £30 and a set of saucepans. After years of protests regarding this clear inequality and discrimination, the imbalance was corrected in 1997 and that same year saw Pete Sampras collect the first of his three consecutive saucepan sets.

* Source: The King's Head, Wimbledon and The Plough Inn, Merton

Photo Credits:

Photos in this book have been supplied by the following photographers and agencies:

007 Magazine Archive: page 15

British Images: pages 3, 7, 38, 40, 47, 91

Gareth Buddo: pages 5, 22, 23, 34, 56, 60, 68

Fotoalia: pages 19, 36, 51, 72

Ned Hoste: pages 18, 48, 78

iStockphoto: pages 4, 6, 8, 9, 10, 11, 14, 15, 16, 20, 21, 26, 28, 29, 31, 32, 33, 35, 37, 39, 40, 41, 44, 45, 46, 47, 49, 50, 61, 64, 65, 67, 73, 76, 79, 81, 82, 83, 84, 85, 87, 90, 93, 94

Mirrorpix: pages 12, 17, 63, 79, 95

Movie Quest Archive: page: 25

Phil Searle, digitalscape: page 13

Photoalto: page 55,

Photodisc: pages 57, 62, 69, 70, 71, 73, 74, 75, 86, 87

Stock.xchng: pages 30 (star-one), 58 (Richard Sweet), 77 (Susana Castillo)

Stockxpert.com: pages 27, 61

Topfoto: pages 43, 53, 59, 89

Virtualbrum.co.uk: page 52